I have a uniform.

I have a hat.

I am a baseball player.

I have a game.

We have fans.

The fans have food.

I have to bat.

Let's play ball.

Sight words are words that occur frequently in stories and text. Typically, these words cannot be sounded out. To develop reading fluency, children need to be able to recognize these words automatically.

Sight word introduced in this book: have

Sight words reviewed in this book: a, I, am, we

Word families reviewed in this book: -an, -at

Ways to use this book:

- Ask your student to read the book aloud. Make sure that he is using the picture above the unknown word to help him figure it out.

- To build fluency, have your child read this book to as many people as possible. It may also be fun to read to a favorite family pet!

Discussion questions:

- Have you ever played baseball?

- What equipment did the baseball player need to play in the game?

- If you had to pick a name for the baseball team in this book, what would it be?

- Some sports are played with teams and some sports are played alone. Can you think of 3 other sports that need to have a team to be played?

Making connections:

Extra Practice: Write the sight word **have** using large letters on a piece of paper. Using different-colored crayons, your kindergartener can then trace the word again and again, reading the word each time.

Get Ready For Dinner

by Mary Poe

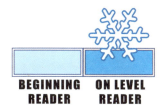

BEGINNING
READER

ON LEVEL
READER

little
lincoln

I can get the napkins.

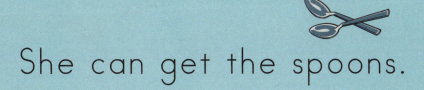

She can get the spoons.

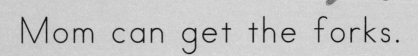

Mom can get the forks.

Dad can get the knives.

I can get the plates.

He can get the glasses.

We set the table.

Let's eat!

Sight words are words that occur frequently in stories and text. Typically, these words cannot be sounded out. To develop reading fluency, children need to be able to recognize these words automatically.

Sight word introduced in this book: get

Sight word reviewed in this book: the, I, she, he, we

Ways to use this book:

- Before he reads the sentence on each page, ask your kindergartener to point to the new sight word. Ask him if there are any other sight words on the page.

- Encourage your reader to point to each word as he reads it. This will give you an idea of how well he tracks print.

Discussion questions:

- What holiday is the family in the story celebrating?

- Besides setting the table, what are some ways that you could help your family on Thanksgiving?

Making connections:

Social Studies: Discuss with your family ways that each person could help out on Thanksgiving. Help your kindergartener to make a list of family members and the way that each will help out on Thanksgiving.

Making connections:

Extra Practice: Sight words can be found in many places. Look in your student's favorite book for the word **get**. When you come to that word in a story, let your student read it. Try doing this activity with other sight words.

Have your student review past sight words by reading the sight word books that have already been introduced.

The Street

by Mary Poe

BEGINNING
READER

ON LEVEL
READER

little
lincoln

He is walking.

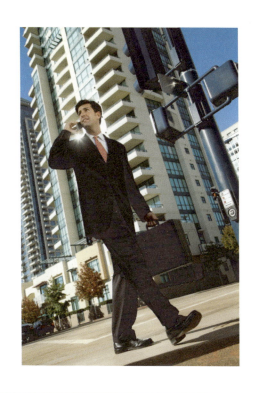

He looks left.

He sees a car.

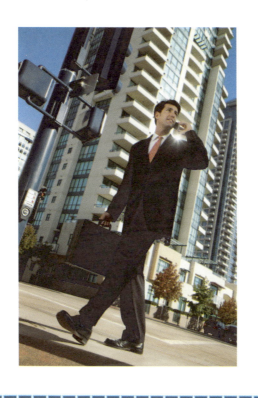

He looks right.

 He sees a car.

He waits.

He can cross.

He is safe.

Sight words are words that occur frequently in stories and text. Typically, these words cannot be sounded out. To develop reading fluency, children need to be able to recognize these words automatically.

Sight word introduced in this book: he

Sight words reviewed in this book: a, is

Word family reviewed in this book: -an

Ways to use this book:

- Before he reads the sentence on each page, ask your student to point to the new sight word. Ask him if there are any other sight words on the page. Continue by asking if there are any unknown words. Review the unknown word before reading the page.

- Encourage your reader to point to each word as he reads it. This will give you an idea of how well he tracks print.

Discussion questions:

- What rules do you need to remember when crossing the street?

- Did the character follow those safety rules?

- Talk about other times when you might have to follow safety rules.

Making connections:

Social Studies: In this story, you learned about safety rules to follow when crossing the street. Discuss with your student rules to follow in other situations. For example: going to the park, going to the pool, riding a bike.

Making connections:

Oral
Communication: Look through books for male characters. When you find
one, ask your kindergartener to tell what he is doing. Make
sure that he responds by saying, "He is...."

Extra Practice: Sight words can be found in many places. Look in your
student's favorite book for the word **he**. When you come to
that word in a story, let your student read it. Try doing this
activity with other sight words.

Give your student the following letter cards: a, b, e, h, I, m,
o, r, s, t, w, y. Show your student the sight word card for **he**
and have him use his letters to spell the word. Continue
with the word cards for a, the, so, am , be , was, my, I, is,
are.

Make the word **he**! Have an adult write the word **he** on a
piece of paper. The kindergartener can then use a bingo
stamper or stickers to "write" or "stamp out" the word **he**.

Sounds

by Mary Poe

BEGINNING READER   ON LEVEL READER

little lincoln

A dog **can** .

The baby can .

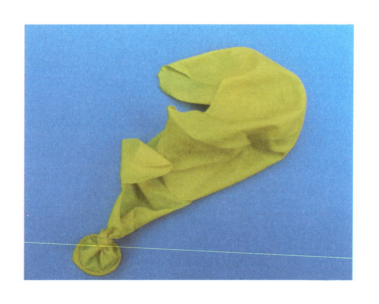

A balloon can .

A cat can .

My dad **can**  .

I can  .

Sight words are words that occur frequently in stories and text. Typically, these words cannot be sounded out. To develop reading fluency, children need to be able to recognize these words automatically.

Sight word introduced in this book: can

Sight word reviewed in this book: a, the, I, my

Ways to use this book:

- Take time to review that a sentence begins with a capital letter and ends with a period. Have your student find the beginning and end of the sentence on each page.

Discussion questions:

- What sounds did you read about in this book?

- Can you think of other sounds that you can hear? What are they?

Making connections:

Oral Communication:

Have your kindergartener close his eyes. While his eyes are closed, you will need to make a sound. Your student will need to guess what the sound was. For example, close a door, run water from a faucet, hit a pan with a spoon.

Extra Practice:

Have your student use a wet sponge or paint brush and write the word **can** on a small chalkboard. The word will magically disappear when it dries. Try asking him to spell other sight words.

Thanksgiving Dinner

by Mary Poe

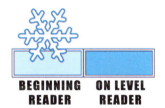

BEGINNING
READER

ON LEVEL
READER

little
lincoln

Get the  .

Get the .

Get the ✕ .

Get the .

Get the  .

Let's eat!

Sight words are words that occur frequently in stories and text. Typically, these words cannot be sounded out. To develop reading fluency, children need to be able to recognize these words automatically.

Sight word introduced in this book: get

Sight word reviewed in this book: the

Ways to use this book:

- Before he reads the sentence on each page, ask your kindergartener to point to the new sight word. Ask him if there are any other sight words on the page.

- Encourage your reader to point to each word as he reads it. This will give you an idea of how well he tracks print.

Discussion questions:

- What holiday is the family in the story celebrating?

- Besides setting the table, what are some ways that you could help your family on Thanksgiving?

Making connections:

Social Studies: Discuss with your family ways that each person could help out on Thanksgiving. Help your kindergartener to make a list of family members and the way that each will help out on Thanksgiving.

Making connections:

Extra Practice: Sight words can be found in many places. Look in your student's favorite book for the word **get**. When you come to that word in a story, let your student read it. Try doing this activity with other sight words.

Have your student review past sight words by reading the sight word books that have already been introduced.

little lincoln

<u>Week 10</u>
Sight word: **At**
Beginning Reader: *At The Carnival*
On Level Reader: *At The Carnival*

Sight word: **He**
Beginning Reader: *Crossing The Street*
On Level Reader: *The Street*

<u>Week 11</u>
Sight word: **Like**
Beginning Reader: *I Like Food*
On Level Reader: *I Like Food*

Sight word: **She**
Beginning Reader: *Community Helpers*
On Level Reader: *Community Helpers*

<u>Week 12</u>
Sight word: **Can**
Beginning Reader: *Sounds*
On Level Reader: *Sounds I Hear*

Sight word: **Get**
Beginning Reader: *Thanksgiving Dinner*
On Level Reader: *Get Ready For Dinner*

<u>Week 13</u>
Sight word: **Have**
Beginning Reader: *The Game*
On Level Reader: *The Baseball Game*

Sight word: **That**
Beginning Reader: *Opposites*
On Level Reader: *Opposites*

<u>Week 14</u>
Sight word: **But**
Beginning Reader: *Food I Like*
On Level Reader: *Food That I Like*

Sight word: **Said**
Beginning Reader: *I Can*
On Level Reader: *Playing Outside*

<u>Week 15</u>
Sight word: **Big**
Beginning Reader: *Big Moves*
On Level Reader: *Sam's Big Truck*

Sight word: **Look**
Beginning Reader: *Look At Us*
On Level Reader: *The Big Show*

<u>Week 16</u>
Sight word: **No**
Beginning Reader: *No, no, Kip!*
On Level Reader: *No, no, Kip!*

Sight word: **Yes**
Beginning Reader: *What Is It?*
On Level Reader: *The Pig*

<u>Week 17</u>
Sight word: **Of**
Beginning Reader: *My Room*
On Level Reader: *In My Room*

Sight word: **This**
Beginning Reader: *Transportation*
On Level Reader: *Transportation*

<u>Week 18</u>
Sight word: **Do**
Beginning Reader: *Winter Sports*
On Level Reader: *Winter Sports*

Sight word: **To**
Beginning Reader: *On Snowy Days*
On Level Reader: *On Snowy Days*

little lincoln

Little Lincoln Kindergarten Sight Word Books

This season, your student will be introduced to eighteen new sight words. Sight words are words that occur frequently in stories and text. Typically, these words cannot be sounded out. To develop reading fluency, children need to be able to recognize these words automatically.

The sight word books for each word are provided at two levels: Beginning Reader and On Level Reader. The level is clearly designated on the front of the book by the appropriate seasonal icon. If your student can easily read the Beginning Reader book, then challenge your student to try reading the On Level Reader book for the same word. Both versions teach the same sight word, but the On Level Reader book is longer and includes more sentences.

Once your student is reading the Beginning Reader books fluently, you may wish to solely focus on the On Level Reader books. Keep in mind that you can go back to the Beginning Reader books at any time, based on your student's needs and abilities. Note that the student does not have to read both levels of each book.

Sounds I Hear

by Mary Poe

BEGINNING READER · ON LEVEL READER

little lincoln

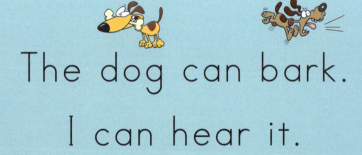

The dog can bark.
I can hear it.

The baby can cry.

I can hear it.

A balloon can pop.

I can hear it.

A cat can meow.

I can hear it.

My dad can laugh.

I can hear it.

The plate can break.

I can hear it.

A whistle blows.

I can hear it.

I can sing.

Can you hear me?

Sight words are words that occur frequently in stories and text. Typically, these words cannot be sounded out. To develop reading fluency, children need to be able to recognize these words automatically.

Sight word introduced in this book: can

Sight word reviewed in this book: a, the, I, my

Ways to use this book:

- Take time to review that a sentence begins with a capital letter and ends with a period. Have your student find the beginning and end of the sentence on each page.

Discussion questions:

- What sounds did you read about in this book?

- Can you think of other sounds that you can hear? What are they?

Making connections:

Oral Communication: Have your kindergartener close his eyes. While his eyes are closed, you will need to make a sound. Your student will need to guess what the sound was. For example, close a door, run water from a faucet, hit a pan with a spoon.

Extra Practice: Have your student use a wet sponge or paint brush and write the word **can** on a small chalkboard. The word will magically disappear when it dries. Try asking him to spell other sight words.

I Can

by Mary Poe

BEGINNING READER **ON LEVEL READER**

little lincoln

"I can," **said** Pat.

"I can," **said** Dan.

"I can," **said** Sam.

"I can," **said** Nan.

"I can," I **said**.

You can too!

Sight words are words that occur frequently in stories and text. Typically, these words cannot be sounded out. To develop reading fluency, children need to be able to recognize these words automatically.

Sight word introduced in this book: said

Sight words reviewed in this book: I, can

Word families reviewed in this book: -an, -at, -am

Ways to use this book:

- Have your student use his index fingers to "frame" a sentence in this book. Have him frame a word that he can read on each page.

Discussion questions:

- What outside activities do you remember reading about in this book?

- What other activities could you do outside?

Making connections:

Math: Create an obstacle course in your backyard or at a local playground. Using a piece of paper, map out where to start and how to go through the course. Once everyone understands how to go through the obstacle course, get out a stop watch and time each person as they complete the course.

Extra Practice: Play Sight Word Go-Fish! Have your student pick 10 known sight words. Each of the sight words will need to be written one time on two index cards (10 words x 2 cards ea. = 20 cards). Deal 5 cards out to each player and have the remaining cards be the "draw" pile. Follow standard "Go-Fish" rules and have fun.

On Snowy Days

by Mary Poe

BEGINNING
READER

ON LEVEL
READER

little
lincoln

On snowy days, I like to sled.

On snowy days, I like

to make a snowman.

On snowy days, I like to ice skate.

On snowy days, I like to make snow angels.

I can make snowballs on snowy days.

What do you do on snowy days?

Sight words are words that occur frequently in stories and text. Typically, these words cannot be sounded out. To develop reading fluency, children need to be able to recognize these words automatically.

Sight word introduced in this book: to

Sight words reviewed in this book: I, like, can, a, do

Ways to use this book:

- Take time to review that a sentence begins with a capital letter and ends with a period. Have your child find the beginning and end of the sentence on each page.

- Have your student count how many words are in each sentence.

Discussion questions:

- The child in this book likes to do many different activities when it snows. What kinds of activities do you like to do when it snows?

- Compare the child in this book to yourself. How are you like the character? How are you different?

Making connections:

Extra Practice: Have your student use a wet sponge or paint brush and write the word **to** on a small chalkboard. The word will magically disappear when it dries. Try asking him to spell other sight words.

Sight words can be found in many places. Look in your child's favorite book for the word **to**. When you come to that word in a story, let your student read it. Try doing this activity with other sight words.

At The Carnival

by Mary Poe

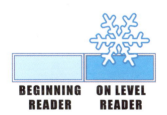

BEGINNING READER   ON LEVEL READER

little lincoln

We are at the carnival.

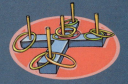

Nan is at a game.

I am at the ride.

A line at the food stand.

Dan is at the ferris wheel.

In my van at night.

I am at home.

Sight words are words that occur frequently in stories and text. Typically, these words cannot be sounded out. To develop reading fluency, children need to be able to recognize these words automatically.

Sight word introduced in this book: at

Sight word reviewed in this book: are, the, is, a, I, am, my

Word family reviewed in this book: -an

Ways to use this book:

- Before he reads the sentence on each page, ask your kindergartener to point to the new sight word. Ask him if there are any other sight words on the page. Continue by asking if there are any unknown words. Review the unknown word before reading the page.

- Encourage your reader to point to each word as he reads it. This will give you an idea of how well he tracks print.

Discussion questions:

- The story that you just read was about a carnival. What carnival activities did you just read about?

- Have you ever been to a carnival before? If so, how was that carnival like the one in this story? How was it different from the carnival in this story?

at

Making connections:

Plan a mini-carnival in your home. Set up a few small carnival games like a bean-bag toss or potato sack race. You may even want to turn your kitchen into a food stand. Once everything is set up, invite some friends over and have a blast at your Kindergarten Carnival.

Extra Practice: Sight words can be found in many places. Look in your student's favorite book for the word **at**. When you come to that word in a story, let your student read it. Try doing this activity with other sight words.

Give your student the following letter cards: a, b, e, h, I, m, o, s, t, w, y. Show your student the sight word card for **at** and have him use his letters to spell the word. Continue with the word cards for a, the, so, am , be , was, my, I, is, are.

Transportation

by Mary Poe

BEGINNING READER   ON LEVEL READER

little lincoln

This is a bike.

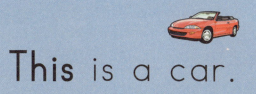

This is a car.

This is a bus.

This **is** a train.

This is a plane.

I can go!

Sight words are words that occur frequently in stories and text. Typically, these words cannot be sounded out. To develop reading fluency, children need to be able to recognize these words automatically.

Sight word introduced in this book: this

Sight words reviewed in this book: is, a, can, I

Ways to use this book:

- Before he reads the sentence on each page, ask your kindergartener to point to the new sight word. Ask him if there are any other sight words on the page.

- Encourage your reader to point to each word as he reads it. This will give you an idea of how well he tracks print.

Discussion questions:

- What modes of transportation did you read about in this book?

- Which types of transportation have you used before? Talk about your experience(s).

Making connections:

Extra Practice: Give your student letter tiles and a list of sight words. Have him use the letters to spell the words. Once a word is completed, make sure to ask, "What word did you spell?"

Winter Sports

by Mary Poe

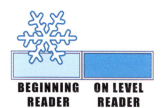

BEGINNING READER   ON LEVEL READER

little lincoln

Do you like to ski?

Yes, I do like to ski.

Do you like to ice skate?

Yes, I do like to ice skate.

Do you like to sled ride?

Yes, I do like to sled ride.

I like to do any winter sport!

Sight words are words that occur frequently in stories and text. Typically, these words cannot be sounded out. To develop reading fluency, children need to be able to recognize these words automatically.

Sight word introduced in this book: do

Sight words reviewed in this book: to, I, yes, like

Ways to use this book:

- Take time to review that a sentence begins with a capital letter and ends with punctuation. There are many different types of punctuation in this book. Take this opportunity to review the period, question mark, and exclamation point. Have your student find the beginning and end of the sentence on each page. Have him tell you the type of punctuation used in that sentence.

Discussion questions:

- What was the setting of this story?

- Tell what happened in the beginning, middle, and end of the story.

Making connections:

Extra Practice: Write the sight word **do** using large letters on a piece of paper. Using different-colored crayons, your kindergartener can then trace the word again and again, reading the word each time.

What Is It?

by Mary Poe

BEGINNING READER **ON LEVEL READER**

little lincoln

Is it pink ?

Yes, it is pink.

Is it big?

Yes, it is big.

Is it a pig?

Yes, it is a pig.

Sight words are words that occur frequently in stories and text. Typically, these words cannot be sounded out. To develop reading fluency, children need to be able to recognize these words automatically.

Sight word introduced in this book: yes

Sight words reviewed in this book: is, a

Word family reviewed in this book: -ig

Ways to use this book:

- Ask your student to read the book aloud. If your child has difficulty reading the words, encourage him to look at the pictures. Many times, the pictures can help him figure out unknown words.

- Many of the sentences in this book end in a question mark. Have your student find the question marks throughout the story.

Discussion questions:

- What -ig word family words did you read in this book? Can you think of other -ig family words?

- Ask your reading partner other yes/no questions about pigs.

Making connections:

Extra Practice: Building fluency: Write each sentence from the book on an index card. Mix up the index cards. Place the cards in a pile face down. Pick a card from the top and read the sentence.

Challenge: Can you put the sentence cards in the correct order?

No, no, Kip!

by Mary Poe

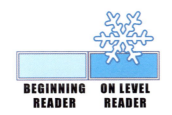

BEGINNING READER   ON LEVEL READER

No, no, Kip!

You cannot dig in the garden.

No, no, Kip!

You cannot eat the flowers.

No, no, Kip!

You cannot run away.

No, you are not bad, Kip.

You are a good dog!

Sight words are words that occur frequently in stories and text. Typically, these words cannot be sounded out. To develop reading fluency, children need to be able to recognize these words automatically.

Sight word introduced in this book: no

Sight words reviewed in this book: can, the, are, a

Word family reviewed in this book: -ip, -ig, -at

Ways to use this book:

- To build fluency, have your child read this book to as many people as possible. It may also be fun to read to a favorite family pet!

Discussion questions:

- What did Kip do that he was not supposed to?

- Why did Kip's owner not want him to dig in the garden?

- Can you think of something else that Kip might do to make his owner say, "No, no, Kip!"?

Making connections:

Visual Arts: Draw a picture that shows Kip doing something that will make his owner say, "No, no, Kip!"

Extra Practice: Write or type simple sentences using known sight words. Have the student practice reading these sentences to build fluency.

Community Helpers

by Mary Poe

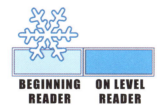

BEGINNING
READER

ON LEVEL
READER

little
lincoln

She is a  .

She is a  .

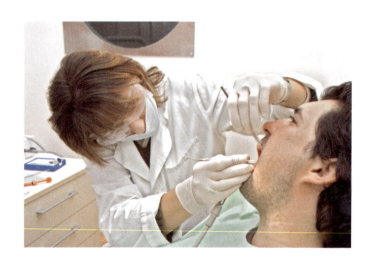

She is a  .

She is a  .

She is a  .

They help.

Sight words are words that occur frequently in stories and text. Typically, these words cannot be sounded out. To develop reading fluency, children need to be able to recognize these words automatically.

Sight word introduced in this book: she

Sight word reviewed in this book: a, is

Ways to use this book:

- Before he reads the sentence on each page, ask your kindergartener to point to the new sight word. Ask him if there are any other sight words on the page.

- Encourage your reader to point to each word as he reads it. This will give you an idea of how well he tracks print.

Discussion questions:

- Who were the characters in the book?
- What jobs did the characters have?
- Name three other helpers in your community.

Making connections:

Social Studies: Make a poster or a collage that shows different community helpers in your neighborhood.

Oral Communication: Look through books for female characters. When you find one, ask your kindergartener to tell what she is doing. Make sure that he responds by saying, "She is...."

Making connections:

Extra Practice: Sight words can be found in many places. Look in your student's favorite book for the word **she**. When you come to that word in a story, let your student read it. Try doing this activity with other sight words.

Using sandpaper and scissors, make the letters s, h, e. Have your student use the sandpaper letters to spell the word she. He can then trace each letter with his finger while saying the name of the letter. This is a wonderful tactile activity for reviewing learned sight words.

No, no, Kip!

by Mary Poe

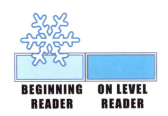

BEGINNING READER   **ON LEVEL READER**

little
lincoln

No, no, Kip!

No digging.

No, no, Kip!

No eating.

No, no, Kip!

No running.

Good boy, Kip!

Sight words are words that occur frequently in stories and text. Typically, these words cannot be sounded out. To develop reading fluency, children need to be able to recognize these words automatically.

Sight word introduced in this book: no

Word family reviewed in this book: -ip

Ways to use this book:

- To build fluency, have your child read this book to as many people as possible. It may also be fun to read to a favorite family pet!

Discussion questions:

- What did Kip do that he was not supposed to?

- Why did Kip's owner not want him to dig in the garden?

- Can you think of something else that Kip might do to make his owner say, "No, no, Kip!"?

Making connections:

Visual Arts: Draw a picture that shows Kip doing something that will make his owner say, "No, no, Kip!"

Extra Practice: Write or type simple sentences using known sight words. Have the student practice reading these sentences to build fluency.

Look At Us

by Mary Poe

BEGINNING READER   **ON LEVEL READER**

little
lincoln

Look at Dan on stage.

Look at Dan sing.

Look at Pat on stage.

Look at Pat dance.

Look at the children on stage.

It looks like fun.

Sight words are words that occur frequently in stories and text. Typically, these words cannot be sounded out. To develop reading fluency, children need to be able to recognize these words automatically.

Sight word introduced in this book: look

Sight words reviewed in this book: at, the, like

Word family reviewed in this book: -at, -an

Ways to use this book:

- Take a "picture walk" through the book before reading it. Remind your student that a picture walk means that you will look at the pictures first without reading the words. Have your student tell you the setting of the story. Ask him what he thinks the book will be about.

Discussion questions:

- Who are the characters in the story?

- Can you retell this story using your own words?

- Have you ever had a performance where you were on a stage? Talk about it.

Making connections:

Dramatic Arts: Take some time to create your own performance. Set up an area of the house that can be the stage. Decide who will perform and what they will do. Don't forget to rehearse a few times! Then sit back, relax, and enjoy the show.

Extra Practice: On the floor or a table, lay out many different letters of the alphabet. Give your student a list of sight words. One at a time, have him use the letters to spell a sight word.

Food That I Like

by Mary Poe

BEGINNING READER   ON LEVEL READER

little lincoln

I like hotdogs, but
not hamburgers.

Pat likes hamburgers,

but not hotdogs.

Dan likes eggs,

but not bacon.

I like bacon,

but not eggs.

Nan likes the peach,
but not the pit.

I like peanut butter,

but not jelly.

She likes peanut butter

and jelly.

What do you like?

Sight words are words that occur frequently in stories and text. Typically, these words cannot be sounded out. To develop reading fluency, children need to be able to recognize these words automatically.

Sight word introduced in this book: but

Sight words reviewed in this book: like, I, she, the

Word families reviewed in this book: -an, -at

Ways to use this book:

- Play Word Detective: Before your kindergartener reads this book for the first time, have him be a detective and find the word **but** each time it appears on a page.

Discussion questions:

- You read about many different types of foods that go together like bacon and eggs. Can you think of other foods that go together?

Making connections:

Oral Communication:	Dramatic Play: Start your own pretend restaurant. Have your student be the waiter and you can be the guest. It may also be fun to switch roles.
Extra Practice:	If weather permits, play sight word hopscotch outside. Use sidewalk chalk to create the hopscotch grid. Write a sight word in each square. Your student must be able to read the sight word before hopping into each square. If weather does not permit you to enjoy this activity outside, try writing the sight words on index cards. Tape each card to the floor and have your student read the card before hopping onto it.

Community Helpers

by Mary Poe

BEGINNING READER   ON LEVEL READER

little
lincoln

She is a police officer.
She helps.

She is a nurse.
She helps.

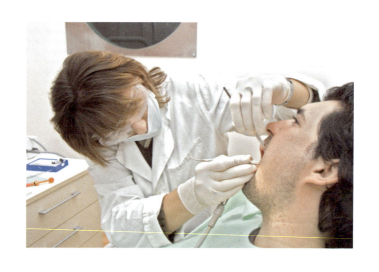

She is a dentist.
She helps.

She is a baker.
She helps.

She is a vet.
She helps.

She is a crossing guard.
She helps.

She is my mom.

She can help.

Sight words are words that occur frequently in stories and text. Typically, these words cannot be sounded out. To develop reading fluency, children need to be able to recognize these words automatically.

Sight word introduced in this book: she

Sight word reviewed in this book: a, is

Word family reviewed in this book: -an

Ways to use this book:

- Before he reads the sentence on each page, ask your kindergartener to point to the new sight word. Ask him if there are any other sight words on the page.

- Encourage your reader to point to each word as he reads it. This will give you an idea of how well he tracks print.

Discussion questions:

- Who were the characters in the book?

- What jobs did the characters have?

- Name three other helpers in your community.

Making connections:

Social Studies: Make a poster or a collage that shows different community helpers in your neighborhood.

Oral Communication: Look through books for female characters. When you find one, ask your kindergartener to tell what she is doing. Make sure that he responds by saying, "She is...."

10

Making connections:

Extra Practice: Sight words can be found in many places. Look in your student's favorite book for the word **she**. When you come to that word in a story, let your student read it. Try doing this activity with other sight words.

Using sandpaper and scissors, make the letters s, h, e. Have your student use the sandpaper letters to spell the word she. He can then trace each letter with his finger while saying the name of the letter. This is a wonderful tactile activity for reviewing learned sight words.

Opposites

by Mary Poe

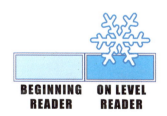

BEGINNING
READER

ON LEVEL
READER

little
lincoln

That fire is hot.

That igloo is cold.

 That toy is new.

 That bear is old.

3

That jet is up.

That car is down.

That is a smile.

That is a frown.

That rabbit is fast.

That turtle is slow.

That is all.

I have to go.

Sight words are words that occur frequently in stories and text. Typically, these words cannot be sounded out. To develop reading fluency, children need to be able to recognize these words automatically.

Sight word introduced in this book: that

Sight words reviewed in this book: is, I, have, a

Ways to use this book:

- Have your student use his index fingers to "frame" a sentence in this book. Have him frame a word that he can read on each page.

Discussion questions:

- In this book, you read about opposites. What is the opposite of fast? Continue with cold and new.
- Besides a fire and an igloo, what other pictures could have been used for the opposites hot/cold?

Making connections:

Visual Arts:　　Using pictures from magazines, make a book of opposites. Label the top of each page with an opposite pair. Divide the page in half and glue pictures of one opposite on one side and the other opposite on the other side.

Extra Practice:　　Using your finger, "write" a sight word on your student's back. Can he guess the word? Trade places and let your student finger write a word from the list on your back. Continue taking turns tracing and guessing sight words.

Crossing The Street

by Mary Poe

BEGINNING
READER · ON LEVEL
READER

little
lincoln

He walks.

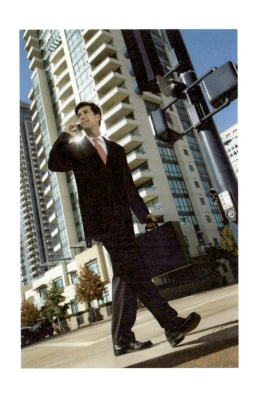

He looks.

A car.

He waits.

He crosses.

He is safe.

Sight words are words that occur frequently in stories and text. Typically, these words cannot be sounded out. To develop reading fluency, children need to be able to recognize these words automatically.

Sight word introduced in this book: he

Sight word reviewed in this book: a

Ways to use this book:

- Before he reads the sentence on each page, ask your student to point to the new sight word. Ask him if there are any other sight words on the page.

- Encourage your reader to point to each word as he reads it. This will give you an idea of how well he tracks print.

Discussion questions:

- What rules do you need to remember when crossing the street?

- Did the character follow those safety rules?

- Talk about other times when you might have to follow safety rules.

Making connections:

Social Studies: In this story, you learned about safety rules to follow when crossing the street. Discuss with your student rules to follow in other situations. For example: going to the park, going to the pool, riding a bike.

Oral Communication: Look through books for male characters. When you find one, ask your kindergartener to tell what he is doing. Make sure that he responds by saying, "He is...."

Making connections:

Extra Practice: Sight words can be found in many places. Look in your student's favorite book for the word **he**. When you come to that word in a story, let your student read it. Try doing this activity with other sight words.

Give your student the following letter cards: a, b, e, h, I, m, o, r, s, t, w, y. Show your student the sight word card for **he** and have him use his letters to spell the word. Continue with the word cards for a, the, so, am , be , was, my, I, is, are.

Make the word **he**! Have an adult write the word **he** on a piece of paper. The kindergartener can then use a bingo stamper or stickers to "write" or "stamp out" the word **he**.

Playing Outside

by Mary Poe

BEGINNING
READER

ON LEVEL
READER

little
lincoln

"I like to hop," said Kit.

"I like to sit," said Nan.

"I like to roll," said Sam.

"I like to run," said Pat.

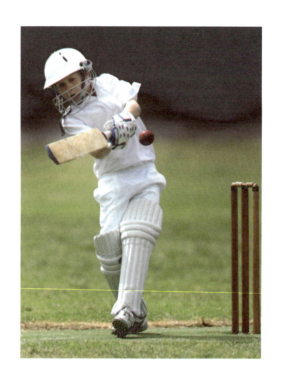

"I like to hit," he said.

What do you like?

We like to play.

Sight words are words that occur frequently in stories and text. Typically, these words cannot be sounded out. To develop reading fluency, children need to be able to recognize these words automatically.

Sight word introduced in this book: said

Sight words reviewed in this book: I, like, he

Word families reviewed in this book: -an, -at, -am, -it

Ways to use this book:

- Have your student use his index fingers to "frame" a sentence in this book. Have him frame a word that he can read on each page.

Discussion questions:

- What outside activities do you remember reading about in this book?

- What other activities could you do outside?

Making connections:

Math: Create an obstacle course in your backyard or at a local playground. Using a piece of paper, map out where to start and how to go through the course. Once everyone understands how to go through the obstacle course, get out a stop watch and time each person as they complete the course.

Extra Practice: Play Sight Word Go-Fish! Have your student pick 10 known sight words. Each of the sight words will need to be written one time on two index cards (10 words x 2 cards ea. = 20 cards). Deal 5 cards out to each player and have the remaining cards be the "draw" pile. Follow standard "Go-Fish" rules and have fun.

I Like Food

by Mary Poe

BEGINNING READER   ON LEVEL READER

little lincoln

I like my pizza.

It is a triangle.

I like my cracker.

It is a square.

I like my cookie.

It is a circle.

I like my chocolate.

It is a rectangle.

I like my cheese.

It is a square.

I like my candy.

It is a circle.

I like my pie.

It is a triangle.

I like food.

Sight words are words that occur frequently in stories and text. Typically, these words cannot be sounded out. To develop reading fluency, children need to be able to recognize these words automatically.

Sight word introduced in this book: like

Sight word reviewed in this book: I, my, is, a

Ways to use this book:

- Look through the book with your kindergartener. Have him point out the sight words on each page. Review any previously learned words.

- Encourage your reader to point to each word as he reads it. This will give you an idea of how well he tracks print.

Discussion questions:

- Can you think of any other foods that are shaped like a square? Continue with circle, triangle, and rectangle.

Making connections:

Visual Arts: Make a shape book. Cut 5 pieces of paper into a circle. These will be your pages. On each page, have your child illustrate one object that is the shape of a circle. Make a cover for your book and staple the pages together. Try making a square book, a triangle book, and a rectangle book.

Making connections:

Science: Spend some time in the kitchen making your favorite food together. Follow the recipe and enjoy your creation.

Extra Practice: Sight words can be found in many places. Look in your student's favorite book for the word **like**. When you come to that word in a story, let your student read it. Try doing this activity with other sight words.

This book talked about food. A fun way to practice spelling the word **like** and other sight words would be to use cooked spaghetti noodles to form the letters of the word.

Transportation

by Mary Poe

BEGINNING
READER

ON LEVEL
READER

little
lincoln

This is my bike.

I can go to the park.

This is a car.

It can go to the library.

This is a bus.

The people can go to the store.

This is a train.

It can go to Grandma's.

This is a plane.

It can fly in the sky.

This is a boat.

The boat can go in the water.

All of these help me go places.

Sight words are words that occur frequently in stories and text. Typically, these words cannot be sounded out. To develop reading fluency, children need to be able to recognize these words automatically.

Sight word introduced in this book: this

Sight words reviewed in this book: is, my, I, can, the

Ways to use this book:

- Before he reads the sentence on each page, ask your kindergartener to point to the new sight word. Ask him if there are any other sight words on the page.

- Encourage your reader to point to each word as he reads it. This will give you an idea of how well he tracks print.

Discussion questions:

- What modes of transportation did you read about in this book?

- Which types of transportation have you used before? Talk about your experience(s).

Making connections:

Extra Practice: Give your student letter tiles and a list of sight words. Have him use the letters to spell the words. Once a word is completed, make sure to ask, "What word did you spell?"

The Pig

by Mary Poe

BEGINNING READER   ON LEVEL READER

little lincoln

Is that his pig?

Yes, that is his pig.

Is the pig pink?

Yes, the pig is pink.

Is the pig big?

Yes, he is very big.

I like the big pig.

Yes, I like him too.

Sight words are words that occur frequently in stories and text. Typically, these words cannot be sounded out. To develop reading fluency, children need to be able to recognize these words automatically.

Sight word introduced in this book: yes

Sight words reviewed in this book: is, that, the,I, like

Word family reviewed in this book: -ig

Ways to use this book:

- Ask your student to read the book aloud. If your child has difficulty reading the words, encourage him to look at the pictures. Many times, the pictures can help him figure out unknown words.

- Many of the sentences in this book end in a question mark. Have your student find the question marks throughout the story.

Discussion questions:

- What -ig word family words did you read in this book? Can you think of other -ig family words?

- Ask your reading partner other yes/no questions about pigs.

Making connections:

Extra Practice: Building fluency: Write each sentence from the book on an index card. Mix up the index cards. Place the cards in a pile face down. Pick a card from the top and read the sentence.

Challenge: Can you put the sentence cards in the correct order?

The Big Show

by Mary Poe

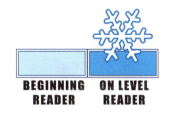

BEGINNING READER   ON LEVEL READER

little lincoln

Look at the children on the stage.

Today is the big show.

Look at Dan on stage.

Look at Dan sing.

He looks happy.

Look at Pat on the stage.

Look at Pat dance.

It looks like fun.

Look at the audience.

They like the big show.

Sight words are words that occur frequently in stories and text. Typically, these words cannot be sounded out. To develop reading fluency, children need to be able to recognize these words automatically.

Sight word introduced in this book: look

Sight words reviewed in this book: at, the, like, she, big, is

Word family reviewed in this book: -at, -an

Ways to use this book:

- Take a "picture walk" through the book before reading it. Remind your student that a picture walk means that you will look at the pictures first without reading the words. Have your student tell you the setting of the story. Ask him what he thinks the book will be about.

Discussion questions:

- Who are the characters in the story?

- Can you retell this story using your own words?

- Have you ever had a performance where you were on a stage? Talk about it.

Making connections:

Dramatic Arts: Take some time to create your own performance. Set up an area of the house that can be the stage. Decide who will perform and what they will do. Don't forget to rehearse a few times! Then sit back, relax, and enjoy the show.

Extra Practice: On the floor or a table, lay out many different letters of the alphabet. Give your student a list of sight words. One at a time, have him use the letters to spell a sight word.

I Like Food

by Mary Poe

BEGINNING READER · ON LEVEL READER

little lincoln

I like pizza.

I like crackers.

I like cookies.

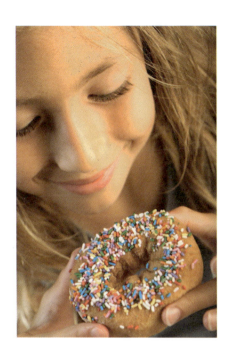

I **like** doughnuts.

I like chocolate.

I like food.

Sight words are words that occur frequently in stories and text. Typically, these words cannot be sounded out. To develop reading fluency, children need to be able to recognize these words automatically.

Sight word introduced in this book: like

Sight word reviewed in this book: I

Ways to use this book:

- Look through the book with your kindergartener. Have him point out the sight words on each page. Review any previously learned words.

- Encourage your reader to point to each word as he reads it. This will give you an idea of how well he tracks print.

Discussion questions:

- The story that you just read was about different kinds of food. Look through the book again and have your kindergartener identify the shape of each type of food.

- Can you think of any other foods that are shaped like a square? Continue with circle, triangle, and rectangle.

Making connections:

Visual Arts: Make a shape book. Cut 5 pieces of paper into a circle. These will be your pages. On each page, have your child illustrate one object that is the shape of a circle. Make a cover for your book and staple the pages together. Try making a square book, a triangle book, and a rectangle book.

Making connections:

Science: Spend some time in the kitchen making your favorite food together. Follow the recipe and enjoy your creation.

Extra Practice: Sight words can be found in many places. Look in your student's favorite book for the word **like**. When you come to that word in a story, let you student read it. Try doing this activity with other sight words.

                     This book talked about food. A fun way to practice spelling the word **like** and other sight words would be to use cooked spaghetti noodles to form the letters of the word.

Sam's Big Truck

by Mary Poe

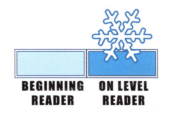

BEGINNING READER   ON LEVEL READER

little lincoln

The rocks are big.

Can we move the big rocks?

Yes, a big truck can move the rocks.

Sam will get his big truck.

Lift the rocks into the big truck.

The truck can move the big rocks.

Sam did it!

 No more big rocks.

Sight words are words that occur frequently in stories and text. Typically, these words cannot be sounded out. To develop reading fluency, children need to be able to recognize these words automatically.

Sight word introduced in this book: big

Sight words reviewed in this book: the, are, can, a, get

Word family reviewed in this book: -am

Ways to use this book:

- Take a "picture walk" through the book before reading it. Remind your student that a picture walk means that you will look at the pictures first without reading the words. Have your student tell you the setting of the story. Ask him what he thinks the book will be about.

Discussion questions:

- What machines helped to move the big items at the construction site?

- Can you think of other machines that can move big things?

Making connections:

Science: Take a trip to a construction site. View the action from afar for you and your student's safety. Have your student see the large machines in action. Discuss how the large machines move the heavy objects.

Extra Practice: Go on a sight word hunt in your home. Have an adult write each sight word on an index card. The adult can then place the cards around your house. Have them tell you a word to hunt for. Go through your home and find that word. Continue until all words have been found.

Big Moves

by Mary Poe

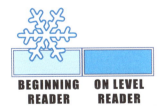

BEGINNING READER   ON LEVEL READER

little lincoln

The rocks are **big**.

 The **big** rocks can be moved.

The logs are **big**.

The **big** logs can be moved.

The bricks are **big**.

The **big** bricks can be moved.

Good job!

Sight words are words that occur frequently in stories and text. Typically, these words cannot be sounded out. To develop reading fluency, children need to be able to recognize these words automatically.

Sight word introduced in this book: big

Sight words reviewed in this book: the, are, can, be

Ways to use this book:

- Take a "picture walk" through the book before reading it. Remind your student that a picture walk means that you will look at the pictures first without reading the words. Have your student tell you the setting of the story. Ask him what he thinks the book will be about.

Discussion questions:

- What machines helped to move the big items at the construction site?

- Can you think of other machines that can move big things?

Making connections:

Science: Take a trip to a construction site. View the action from afar for you and your student's safety. Have your student see the large machines in action. Discuss how the large machines move the heavy objects.

Extra Practice: Go on a sight word hunt in your home. Have an adult write each sight word on an index card. The adult can then place the cards around your house. Have them tell you a word to hunt for. Go through your home and find that word. Continue until all words have been found.

My Room

by Mary Poe

BEGINNING READER   ON LEVEL READER

little lincoln

The bin **of** toys.

A picture **of** me.

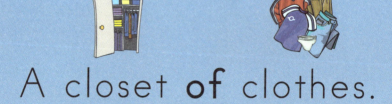

A closet **of** clothes.

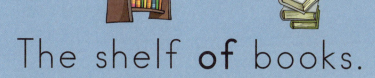

The shelf **of** books.

A pair **of** shoes.

I like my room.

Sight words are words that occur frequently in stories and text. Typically, these words cannot be sounded out. To develop reading fluency, children need to be able to recognize these words automatically.

Sight word introduced in this book: of

Sight words reviewed in this book: the, a, my, like, I

Word family reviewed in this book: -in

Ways to use this book:

- Partner read this book with your student. He can read page 1 and then you read page 2. He reads page 3 and you read page 4. Continue in this manner until the whole book has been read.

Discussion questions:

- The setting of this book was a child's bedroom. What objects were in the room?

- Compare the objects in this room to the objects in your room. What is the same? What is different?

Making connections:

Social Studies: Make a map that illustrates your bedroom or another room in your house. Do not forget to include important objects in the room like the bed or a bookshelf.

Extra Practice: Make a BINGO board that includes some of your student's favorite sight words. Invite different family members to play sight word bingo with your kindergartener.

In My Room

by Mary Poe

BEGINNING READER   ON LEVEL READER

little lincoln

I have a lot in my room.

I have a bin of toys.

And a picture of me.

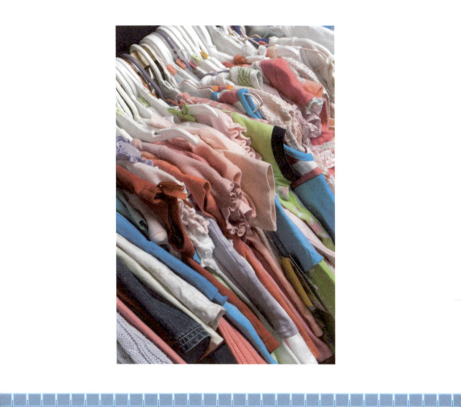

I have a closet of clothes.

And a shelf of books.

I have a pair of shoes.

At the end of the day,
I get in my bed.

Good night!

Sight words are words that occur frequently in stories and text. Typically, these words cannot be sounded out. To develop reading fluency, children need to be able to recognize these words automatically.

Sight word introduced in this book: of

Sight words reviewed in this book: I, have, a, my, at, the, get

Word family reviewed in this book: -in

Ways to use this book:

- Partner read this book with your student. He can read page 1 and then you read page 2. He reads page 3 and you read page 4. Continue in this manner until the whole book has been read.

Discussion questions:

- The setting of this book was a child's bedroom. What objects were in the room?

- Compare the objects in this room to the objects in your room. What is the same? What is different?

Making connections:

Social Studies: Make a map that illustrates your bedroom or another room in your house. Do not forget to include important objects in the room like the bed or a bookshelf.

Extra Practice: Make a BINGO board that includes some of your student's favorite sight words. Invite different family members to play sight word bingo with your kindergartener.

The Game

by Mary Poe

BEGINNING READER   ON LEVEL READER

little lincoln

I have a  .

I have a  .

I have a  .

I have a  .

I have a  .

We have a .

Sight words are words that occur frequently in stories and text. Typically, these words cannot be sounded out. To develop reading fluency, children need to be able to recognize these words automatically.

Sight word introduced in this book: have

Sight words reviewed in this book: a, I, we

Ways to use this book:

- Ask your student to read the book aloud. Make sure that he is using the picture above the unknown word to help him figure it out.

- To build fluency, have your child read this book to as many people as possible. It may also be fun to read to a favorite family pet!

Discussion questions:

- Have you ever played baseball?

- What equipment did the baseball player need to play in the game?

- If you had to pick a name for the baseball team in this book, what would it be?

- Some sports are played with teams and some sports are played alone. Can you think of 3 other sports that need to have a team to be played?

Making connections:

Extra Practice: Write the sight word **have** using large letters on a piece of paper. Using different-colored crayons, your kindergartener can then trace the word again and again, reading the word each time.

Food I Like

by Mary Poe

BEGINNING READER   ON LEVEL READER

little lincoln

I like ,

but not .

I like ,

but not .

I like  ,

6

but not  .

Sight words are words that occur frequently in stories and text. Typically, these words cannot be sounded out. To develop reading fluency, children need to be able to recognize these words automatically.

Sight word introduced in this book: but

Sight words reviewed in this book: like, I

Ways to use this book:

- Play Word Detective: Before your kindergartener reads this book for the firs time, have him be a detective and find the word **but** each time it appears or a page.

Discussion questions:

- You read about many different types of foods that go together like bacon an eggs. Can you think of other foods that go together?

Making connections:

Oral Communication:	Dramatic Play: Start your own pretend restaurant. Have your student be the waiter and you can be the guest. It may also be fun to switch roles.
Extra Practice:	If weather permits, play sight word hopscotch outside. Use sidewalk chalk to create the hopscotch grid. Write a sight word in each square. Your student must be able to read the sight word before hopping into each square. If weather does not permit you to enjoy this activity outside, try writing the sight words on index cards. Tape each card to the floor and have your student read the card before hopping onto it.

Winter Sports

by Mary Poe

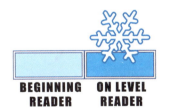

BEGINNING READER   ON LEVEL READER

little lincoln

Do you like to ski?

Yes, I do like to ski.

Do you like to ice skate?

Yes, I do like to ice skate.

Do you like to go sled riding?

Yes, sled riding is so much fun!

Do you like all winter sports?

No, I do not like to snowboard.

At the end of the day,

I like to go in and rest.

Boy, do I like to rest.

Sight words are words that occur frequently in stories and text. Typically, these words cannot be sounded out. To develop reading fluency, children need to be able to recognize these words automatically.

Sight word introduced in this book: do

Sight words reviewed in this book: to, I, is, the, at, of, yes, no, so, like

Ways to use this book:

- Take time to review that a sentence begins with a capital letter and ends with punctuation. There are many different types of punctuation in this book. Take this opportunity to review the period, question mark, and exclamation point. Have your student find the beginning and end of the sentence on each page. Have him tell you the type of punctuation used in that sentence.

Discussion questions:

- What was the setting of this story?

- Tell what happened in the beginning, middle, and end of the story.

Making connections:

Extra Practice: Write the sight word **do** using large letters on a piece of paper. Using different-colored crayons, your kindergartener can then trace the word again and again, reading the word each time.

Opposites

by Mary Poe

BEGINNING
READER

ON LEVEL
READER

little
lincoln

That is hot.

That is cold.

That is new.

That is old.

That is fast.

That is slow.

That is all.
I have to go.

Sight words are words that occur frequently in stories and text. Typically, these words cannot be sounded out. To develop reading fluency, children need to be able to recognize these words automatically.

Sight word introduced in this book: that

Sight words reviewed in this book: is, I, have

Ways to use this book:

- Have your student use his index fingers to "frame" a sentence in this book. Have him frame a word that he can read on each page.

Discussion questions:

- In this book, you read about opposites. What is the opposite of fast? Continue with cold and new.

- Besides a fire and an igloo, what other pictures could have been used for the opposites hot/cold?

Making connections:

Visual Arts: Using pictures from magazines, make a book of opposites. Label the top of each page with an opposite pair. Divide the page in half and glue pictures of one opposite on one side and the other opposite on the other side.

Extra Practice: Using your finger, "write" a sight word on your student's back. Can he guess the word? Trade places and let your student finger write a word from the list on your back. Continue taking turns tracing and guessing sight words.

The Baseball Game

by Mary Poe

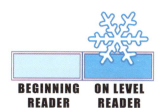

BEGINNING READER   ON LEVEL READER

little lincoln

I have a ball.

I have a bat.